Dear Reader,

A character in one of the stories in this book is upset because he is different from the other children around him. He later learns that what makes him different also makes him special. Just as the sparkling colors in a rainbow are all different, they are alike in their specialness. As you read the literature in this book, think about how people are alike and different. We hope the stories in this book will help you enjoy the different people and wonderful experiences that make our world such a special place.

Sometimes people need to take time out from their busy lives to think about what is important. The stories that follow will introduce you to an African American family that grows closer while working toward a family goal. You'll meet a Native American boy who brings colors to his world. You'll learn about an older Swedish man who meets a difficult challenge even though some people told him he couldn't. You'll also read about some special people who use their time to care for animals in trouble.

As you read the selections in *Sparkling Colors*, think about what's important to you. Reading will help you learn something special about yourself and other people. Poet Myra Cohn Livingston described books this way:

Closed, I am a mystery.
Open, I will always be
a friend with whom you think and see.

Sincerely,
The Authors

SPARKLING·COLORS

CONTENTS

Supergrandpa

by David M. Schwartz   illustrated by Bert Dodson

Gustaf Håkansson was sixty-
six years old. His hair was
snow white. His beard was a
white bush. His face rippled
with wrinkles whenever he
smiled. Gustaf Håkansson
looked like an old man, but
he didn't feel old, and he
certainly didn't act old.

AWARD-WINNING
ILLUSTRATOR

6

Everyone for miles around knew Gustaf.
People saw him on his bicycle, rain or shine,
riding through the crooked streets of
Grantofta—past the baker's and the butcher's
and the wooden-toy maker's, over the stone
bridge leading out of town, up steep hills
scattered with farms, down narrow lanes
bordered by stones, then home again
to his morning paper and a bowl of
sour milk and lingonberries.

One morning Gustaf read something very interesting in the paper. There was going to be a bicycle race called the Tour of Sweden. It would be more than one thousand miles long, and it would last many days.

"This Tour of Sweden is for me!" exclaimed Gustaf.

"But you're too old for a bicycle race," said Gustaf's wife.

"You'll keel over," said his son. "It would be the end of you."

Even his grandchildren laughed at the idea. "You can't ride your bike a thousand miles, Grandpa," they scoffed.

"*Struntprat!*" Gustaf answered. "Silly talk!" And he hopped onto his bike and rode off to see the judges of the race. He would tell them that he planned to enter the Tour of Sweden.

"But this race is for young people," said the first judge. "You're too old, Gustaf."

"You would never make it to the finish," said the second judge.

"We can only admit racers who are strong and fit," said the third judge. "What if you collapsed in the middle of the race?"

"*Struntprat!*" protested Gustaf. "I have no intention of collapsing, because I *am* strong and fit!"

But the judges were not to be moved. "We're sorry, Gustaf," they grumbled. "Go home. Go home to your rocking chair."

Gustaf went home, but he did not go to his rocking chair. "They can keep me out of the race," he muttered, "but they can't keep me off the road."

The next morning, Gustaf began to prepare for the long ride ahead. He arose with the sun, packed some fruit and rye bread, and cycled far out of town—over rolling hills dotted with ancient castles, across valleys dimpled with lakes, through forests thick with birches and pines. It was midafternoon before he returned. The next day he biked even farther. Each day he added more miles to his ride.

A few days before the race, all the young cyclists boarded a special train to Haparanda, in the far north of Sweden, where the race was to begin. But Gustaf was not an official racer. He had no train ticket.

There was only one way for Gustaf to ride in the Tour of Sweden. He would have to pedal six hundred miles to the starting line!

It took him several days to bike there. He arrived just as the Tour of Sweden was about to begin.

All the racers wore numbers, but of course there was no number for Gustaf. So he found a bright red scrap of fabric and made his own.

What number should he be? He had an idea. He wasn't supposed to be in the race at all, so he would be Number Zero!

He chuckled as he cut out a big red zero and pinned it to his shirt. Then he wheeled his bicycle to the starting line.

The starting gun went off and all the young cyclists took off in a spurt. Their legs pumped furiously and their bikes sprinted ahead. They soon left Gustaf far behind.

That night, the racers stopped at an inn. They were treated to dinner and a bed.

Hours later, Gustaf reached the inn too. But there was no bed for him, so he just kept riding. While the others snoozed the night away, Gustaf pedaled into the dawn.

Early the next day, the other cyclists passed Gustaf. But he kept up his steady pace, and late that evening he again overtook the young racers as they rested. In the middle of the night, he napped for three hours on a park bench.

On the third morning, Gustaf was the first to arrive in the little town of Lulea. A small crowd of people waited, hoping to catch a glimpse of the racers zooming by. Instead they saw Gustaf. His white beard fluttered in the breeze. His red cheeks were puffed out with breath. "Look!" cried a little girl. "Look! There goes Supergrandpa!"

"Supergrandpa?" Everyone craned to see.

"Yes, yes, he does look like a Supergrandpa!" A few clapped. Others shouted friendly greetings. Some of the children held out their hands and Gustaf brushed their palms as he rode by. "Thank you, Supergrandpa! Good luck to you."

A photographer snapped Gustaf's picture. It appeared the next day in the newspaper. The headline read: *Supergrandpa Takes a Ride.*

Now all of Sweden knew about Super-grandpa Gustaf Håkansson.

When he got hungry or thirsty, people gave him sour milk with lingonberries, tea and cake, fruit juice, rye bread, or any other snack he wanted.

Newspaper reporters rushed up to talk with him. Radio interviewers broadcast every word he spoke. Everyone wanted to know how he felt.

"I have never felt better in my whole life," he told them.

"But aren't you tired?" they asked.

"How can I be tired when I am surrounded by so much kindness?" And with a push on the pedal and a wave of his hand, Gustaf was rolling down the road again.

Once again Gustaf rode through the night, passing the other racers while they slept. When his muscles felt stiff, he remembered his cheering fans. He pedaled harder.

And so it went, day after night, night after day. By the light of the moon, Gustaf quietly passed the young racers in their beds, then

slept outside, but only for a few hours. Under the long rays of the morning sun, they overtook him and left him struggling to keep up his spirits and his pace. But each day it took them a little longer to catch up with Gustaf.

On the sixth morning of the race, thousands lined the road. As Gustaf rode by, their joyful cheers traveled with him like a wave through the crowd.

"You're almost there, Supergrandpa!"

"A few more miles!"

"Don't look back."

"You're going to win!"

Win? Gustaf hadn't thought about winning. He had simply wanted to ride in the Tour of Sweden and reach the finish line. But win?

"You're out in front, Supergrandpa."

"A few more miles, Supergrandpa, and you'll be the winner!"

The winner? Gustaf glanced over his
shoulder. The pack of racers was catching up.
Their heads and shoulders were hunched low
over their handlebars. Their backs were raised
high above their seats.

Gustaf decided not to think about them.
Instead he thought about his many fans. He
thought about how they wanted him to win. He
And suddenly, he wanted to win too!

Gustaf looked ahead. In the distance he
could see a bright banner stretched all the way
across the road. The finish line!

Gustaf lowered his head. He raised his
back. He whipped his legs around with all
their might and all their motion.

The next time he looked up he was bursting through the banner and rolling over the finish line—just before another racer thundered past.

The crowd roared. People lifted Gustaf onto their shoulders. They showered him with flowers. They sang victory songs. The police band played patriotic marches.

The three judges, however, said that Gustaf could *not* be the winner, because he was never actually in the race. Besides, it was against the rules to ride at night. No, the big gold trophy would go to another racer, not to Gustaf.

But no one seemed to care what the judges said. Even the king stepped up to hug Gustaf and invite him to the palace. And to nearly everyone in Sweden, Gustaf Håkansson— sixty-six years old, his hair as white as snow, his beard a great white bush, his smiling face an orb of wrinkles—to them, Supergrandpa Gustaf Håkansson had won the Tour of Sweden.

a Note from the Author:

David M. Schwartz

There really was a sixty-six-year-old Gustaf Håkansson who, in 1951, rode 1,761 kilometers (1,094 miles) in the *Sverige-Loppet,* the longest bicycle race in the history of Sweden. Cycling day and night, Gustaf did finish first. A little girl who saw the old man on his bike awarded him the name that the rest of the nation adopted, *Stålfarfar.* It means "Steel Grandfather," but since Swedish children call "Superman" *Stålman,* we can translate *Stålfarfar* as "Supergrandpa."

Gustaf's race captured the imagination of his countrymen, and he became a hero.

After the race, admirers wrote to Gustaf from all over Sweden. Not knowing his address or his real name, many just wrote *Stålfarfar* on the envelope. That's all, just *Stålfarfar,* and the post office knew where to deliver the letters! Some people sent Gustaf gifts, such as rocking chairs and mattresses on which to take a well-deserved rest.

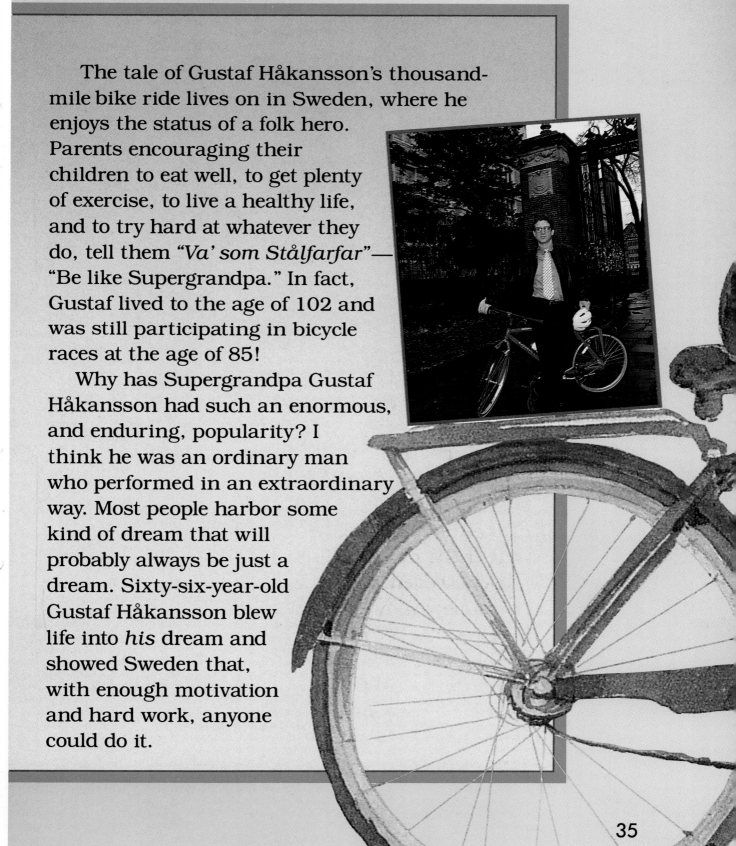

The tale of Gustaf Håkansson's thousand-mile bike ride lives on in Sweden, where he enjoys the status of a folk hero. Parents encouraging their children to eat well, to get plenty of exercise, to live a healthy life, and to try hard at whatever they do, tell them *"Va' som Stålfarfar"*— "Be like Supergrandpa." In fact, Gustaf lived to the age of 102 and was still participating in bicycle races at the age of 85!

Why has Supergrandpa Gustaf Håkansson had such an enormous, and enduring, popularity? I think he was an ordinary man who performed in an extraordinary way. Most people harbor some kind of dream that will probably always be just a dream. Sixty-six-year-old Gustaf Håkansson blew life into *his* dream and showed Sweden that, with enough motivation and hard work, anyone could do it.

35

·THE·
PATCHWORK QUILT
by VALERIE FLOURNOY
pictures by JERRY PINKNEY

FLOURNOY / PINKNEY · THE PATCHWORK QUILT · Dial

Tanya sat restlessly on her chair by the kitchen window. For several days she had had to stay in bed with a cold. But now Tanya's cold was almost gone. She was anxious to go outside and enjoy the fresh air and the arrival of spring.

"Mama, when can I go outside?" asked Tanya. Mama pulled the tray of biscuits from the oven and placed it on the counter.

"In time," she murmured. "All in good time."

Tanya gazed through the window and saw her two brothers, Ted and Jim, and Papa building the new backyard fence.

"I'm gonna talk to Grandma," she said.

Grandma was sitting in her favorite spot—the big soft chair in front of the picture window. In her lap were scraps of materials of all textures and colors. Tanya recognized some of them. The plaid was from Papa's old work shirt, and the red scraps were from the shirt Ted had torn that winter.

"Whatcha gonna do with all that stuff?" Tanya asked.

"Stuff? These ain't stuff. These little pieces gonna make me a quilt, a patchwork quilt."

Tanya tilted her head. "I know what a quilt is, Grandma. There's one on your bed, but it's old and dirty and Mama can never get it clean."

Grandma sighed. "It ain't dirty, honey. It's worn, the way it's supposed to be."

Grandma flexed her fingers to keep them from stiffening. She sucked in some air and said, "My mother made me a quilt when I wasn't any older than you. But sometimes the old ways are forgotten."

Tanya leaned against the chair and rested her head on her grandmother's shoulder.

Just then Mama walked in with two glasses of milk and some biscuits. Mama looked at the scraps of material that were scattered all over. "Grandma," she said, "I just cleaned this room, and now it's a mess."

"It's not a mess, Mama," Tanya said through a mouthful of biscuit. "It's a quilt."

"A quilt! You don't need these scraps. I can get you a quilt," Mama said.

Grandma looked at her daughter and then turned to her grandchild. "Yes, your mama can get you a quilt from any department store. But it won't be like my patchwork quilt, and it won't last as long either."

Mama looked at Grandma, then picked up Tanya's empty glass and went to make lunch.

Grandma's eyes grew dark and distant. She turned away from Tanya and gazed out the window, absentmindedly rubbing the pieces of material through her fingers.

"Grandma, I'll help you make your quilt," Tanya said.

"Thank you, honey."

"Let's start right now. We'll be finished in no time."

Grandma held Tanya close and patted her head. "It's gonna take quite a while to make this quilt, not a couple of days or a week—not even a month. A good quilt, a masterpiece . . ." Grandma's eyes shone at the thought. "Why I need more material. More gold and blue, some red and green. And I'll need the time to do it right. It'll take me a year at least."

"A year," shouted Tanya. "That's too long. I can't wait that long, Grandma."

Grandma laughed. "A year ain't that long, honey. Makin' this quilt gonna be a joy. Now run along and let Grandma rest." Grandma turned her head toward the sunlight and closed her eyes.

"I'm gonna make a masterpiece," she murmured, clutching a scrap of cloth in her hand, just before she fell asleep.

"We'll have to get you a new pair and use these old ones for rags," Mama said as she hung the last piece of wash on the clothesline one August afternoon.

Jim was miserable. His favorite blue corduroy pants had been held together with patches; now they were beyond repair.

"Bring them here," Grandma said.

Grandma took part of the pant leg and cut a few blue squares. Jim gave her a hug and watched her add his patches to the others.

"A quilt won't forget. It can tell your life story," she said.

The arrival of autumn meant school and Halloween. This year Tanya would be an African princess. She danced around in the long, flowing robes Mama had made from several yards of colorful material. The old bracelets and earrings Tanya had found in a trunk in the attic jingled noisily as she moved. Grandma cut some squares out of the leftover scraps and added Tanya to the quilt too!

The days grew colder but Tanya and her brothers didn't mind. They knew snow wasn't far away. Mama dreaded winter's coming. Every year she would plead with Grandma to move away from the drafty window, but Grandma wouldn't budge.

"Grandma, please," Mama scolded. "You can sit here by the heater."

"I'm not your grandmother, I'm your mother," Grandma said. "And I'm gonna sit here in the Lord's light and make my masterpiece."

It was the end of November when Ted, Jim, and Tanya got their wish. They awoke one morning to find everything in sight covered with snow. Tanya got dressed and flew down the stairs. Ted and Jim, and even Mama and Papa, were already outside.

"I don't like leaving Grandma in that house by herself," Mama said. "I know she's lonely."

Tanya pulled herself out of the snow being careful not to ruin her angel. "Grandma isn't lonely," Tanya said happily. "She and the quilt are telling each other stories."

Mama glanced questioningly at Tanya, "Telling each other stories?"

"Yes, Grandma says a quilt never forgets!"

The family spent the morning and most of the afternoon sledding down the hill. Finally, when they were all numb from the cold, they went inside for hot chocolate and sandwiches.

"I think I'll go sit and talk to Grandma," Mama said.

"Then she can explain to you about our quilt—our very own family quilt," Tanya said.

Mama saw the mischievous glint in her youngest child's eyes.

"Why, I may just have her do that, young lady," Mama said as she walked out of the kitchen.

Tanya leaned over the table to see into the living room. Grandma was hunched over, her eyes close to the fabric as she made tiny stitches. Mama sat at the old woman's feet. Tanya couldn't hear what was said but she knew Grandma was telling Mama all about quilts and how *this* quilt would be very special. Tanya sipped her chocolate slowly, then she saw Mama pick up a piece of fabric, rub it with her fingers, and smile.

From that moment on both women spent their winter evenings working on the quilt. Mama did the sewing while Grandma cut the fabrics and placed the scraps in a pattern of colors. Even while they were cooking and baking all their Christmas specialties during the day, at night they still worked on the quilt. Only once did Mama put it aside. She wanted to wear something special Christmas night, so she bought some gold material and made a beautiful dress. Tanya knew without asking that the gold scraps would be in the quilt too.

There was much singing and laughing that Christmas. All Grandma's sons and daughters and nieces and nephews came to pay their respects. The Christmas tree lights shone brightly, filling the room with sparkling colors. Later, when everyone had gone home, Papa said he had never felt so much happiness in the house. And Mama agreed.

When Tanya got downstairs the next morning, she found Papa fixing pancakes.

"Is today a special day too?" asked Jim.

"Where's Mama?" asked Tanya.

"Grandma doesn't feel well this morning," Papa said. "Your mother is with her now till the doctor gets here."

"Will Grandma be all right?" Ted asked.

Papa rubbed his son's head and smiled. "There's nothing for you to worry about. We'll take care of Grandma."

Tanya looked into the living room. There on the back of the big chair rested the patchwork quilt. It was folded neatly, just as Grandma had left it.

"Mother didn't want us to know she wasn't feeling well. She thought it would spoil our Christmas," Mama told them later, her face drawn and tired, her eyes a puffy red. "Now it's up to all of us to be quiet and make her as comfortable as possible." Papa put an arm around Mama's shoulder.

"Can we see Grandma?" Tanya asked.

"No, not tonight," Papa said. "Grandma needs plenty of rest."

It was nearly a week, the day before New Year's, before the children were permitted to see their grandmother. She looked tired and spoke in whispers.

"We miss you, Grandma," Ted said.

"And your muffins and hot chocolate," added Jim. Grandma smiled.

"Your quilt misses you too, Grandma," Tanya said. Grandma's smile faded from her lips. Her eyes grew cloudy.

"My masterpiece," Grandma sighed. "It would have been beautiful. Almost half finished." The old woman closed her eyes and turned away from her grandchildren. Papa whispered it was time to leave. Ted, Jim, and Tanya crept from the room.

Tanya walked slowly to where the quilt lay. She had seen Grandma and Mama work on it. Tanya thought real hard. She knew how to cut the scraps, but she wasn't certain of the rest. Just then Tanya felt a hand resting on her shoulder. She looked up and saw Mama.

"Tomorrow," Mama said.

New Year's Day was the beginning. After the dishes were washed and put away, Tanya and Mama examined the quilt.

"You cut more squares, Tanya, while I stitch some patches together," Mama said.

Tanya snipped and trimmed the scraps of material till her hands hurt from the scissors. Mama watched her carefully, making sure the squares were all the same size. The next day was the same as the last. More snipping and cutting. But Mama couldn't always be around to watch Tanya work. Grandma had to be looked after. So Tanya worked by herself. Then one night, as Papa read them stories, Jim walked over and looked at the quilt. In it he saw patches of blue. His blue. Without saying a word Jim picked up the scissors and some scraps and started to make squares. Ted helped Jim put the squares in piles while Mama showed Tanya how to join them.

Every day, as soon as she got home from school, Tanya worked on the quilt. Ted and Jim were too busy with sports, and Mama was looking after Grandma, so Tanya worked alone. But after a few weeks she stopped. Something was wrong—something was missing, Tanya thought. For days the quilt lay on the back of the chair. No one knew why Tanya had stopped working. Tanya would sit and look at the quilt. Finally she knew. Some*thing* wasn't missing. Some*one* was missing from the quilt.

That evening before she went to bed Tanya tiptoed into Grandma's room, a pair of scissors in her hand. She quietly lifted the end of Grandma's old quilt and carefully removed a few squares.

February and March came and went as Mama proudly watched her daughter work on the last few rows of patches. Tanya always found time for the quilt. Grandma had been watching too. The old woman had been getting stronger and stronger as the months passed. Once she was able, Papa would carry Grandma to her chair by the window. "I needs the Lord's light," Grandma said. Then she would sit and hum softly to herself and watch Tanya work.

"Yes, honey, this quilt is nothin' but a joy," Grandma said.

Summer vacation was almost here. One June day Tanya came home to find Grandma working on the quilt again! She had finished sewing the last few squares together; the stuffing was in place, and she was already pinning on the backing.

"Grandma!" Tanya shouted.

Grandma looked up. "Hush, child. It's almost time to do the quilting on these patches. But first I have some special finishing touches. . . ."

The next night Grandma cut the final thread with her teeth. "There. It's done," she said. Mama helped Grandma spread the quilt full length.

Nobody had realized how big it had gotten or how beautiful. Reds, greens, blues, and golds, light shades and dark, blended in and out throughout the quilt.

"It's beautiful," Papa said. He touched the gold patch, looked at Mama, and remembered. Jim remembered too. There was his blue and the red from Ted's shirt. There was Tanya's Halloween costume. And there was Grandma. Even though her patch was old, it fit right in.

They all remembered the past year. They especially remembered Tanya and all her work. So it had been decided. In the right hand corner of the last row of patches was delicately stitched, "For Tanya from your Mama and Grandma."

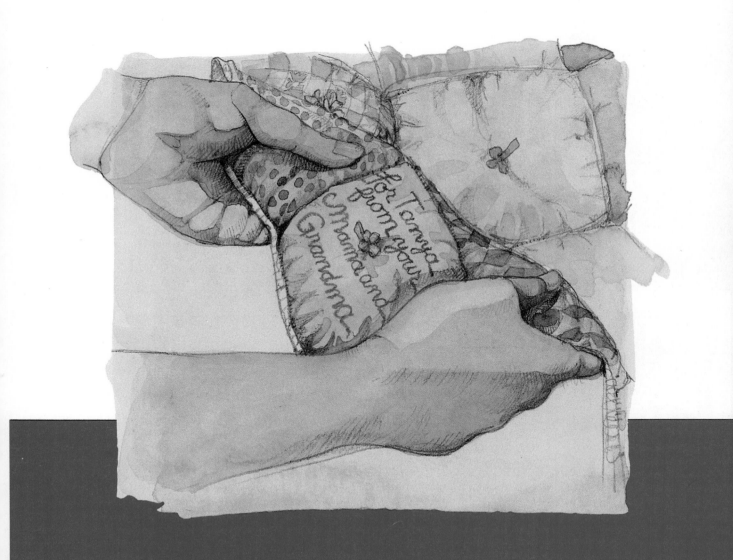

WORDS FROM THE AUTHOR:
Valerie Flournoy

I wrote *The Patchwork Quilt* because I wanted to write a book for my grandmother. She was a quiet, soft-spoken woman with long, frail fingers. She never taught me how to quilt, but she did show us how to make biscuits with a rolling pin and to cut them out with a jelly jar, and how to make apple pies. My middle name is Rose, after her.

I wasn't sure what form my book would take, but one day I was reading an article about quilting, and I decided that quilting would be a good way to talk about family history. Since I wrote this book, I've received lots of letters from kids and their parents who say the story reminds them of their family.

When I go to speak to people, they often bring in their old quilts. Sometimes the classes make their own quilts. They're made out of everything from tissue to felt. I don't quilt, but I've bought several books on quilting, and I'm going to take it up when I have a chance. Also, I've done some research on slavery, and I've learned that the slaves' quilts often contained messages with information about how to get away. That would make an interesting book.

People often think that authors and artists work together, but that's not always the case. The publisher of *The Patchwork Quilt* gave the manuscript to Jerry Pinkney, and I didn't see the pictures until the book was done. I thought they were wonderful! It was almost as if Jerry had been inside my mind and drew what I was able to see. Of all my books, *The Patchwork Quilt* is my favorite.

You have just read a story illustrated by Jerry Pinkney. Here's what Mr. Pinkney has to say about how he creates pictures for books.

WORDS FROM THE ILLUSTRATOR:
Jerry Pinkney

AWARD-WINNING ILLUSTRATOR

Question: Do you use models for the main characters in the books you illustrate?

Answer: Yes.

Question: Who were the models for the characters in *The Patchwork Quilt*?

Answer: I modeled the father in the story after myself. My wife, Gloria, was the model for Tanya's mother. The models for Tanya and her grandmother were two friends of mine, Shondell and Sophie.

Question: Did you have to do research to find out how Tanya's African princess costume should look?

Answer: Yes, I did research.

Question: Does an African princess really wear what Tanya wore?

Answer: The fabric for Tanya's costume is African.

Question: How did you decide on the illustration for the cover of the book?

Answer: I used the main characters in the story—Tanya and her grandmother—and the quilt, of course. I also tried to show the warmth and affection Tanya and her grandmother have for each other.

Question: What is the most enjoyable part of being a children's book illustrator?

Answer: For me it is when the art is finished and I receive the published book in the mail. It is very exciting to open a new book that I have illustrated.

A CHAIR FOR MY MOTHER

written and illustrated by Vera B. Williams

CALDECOTT HONOR

BOSTON GLOBE-HORN BOOK AWARD

My mother works as a waitress in the Blue Tile Diner. After school sometimes I go to meet her there. Then her boss Josephine gives me a job too.

I wash the salts and peppers and fill the ketchups. One time I peeled all the onions for the onion soup. When I finish, Josephine says, "Good work, honey," and pays me. And every time, I put half of my money into the jar.

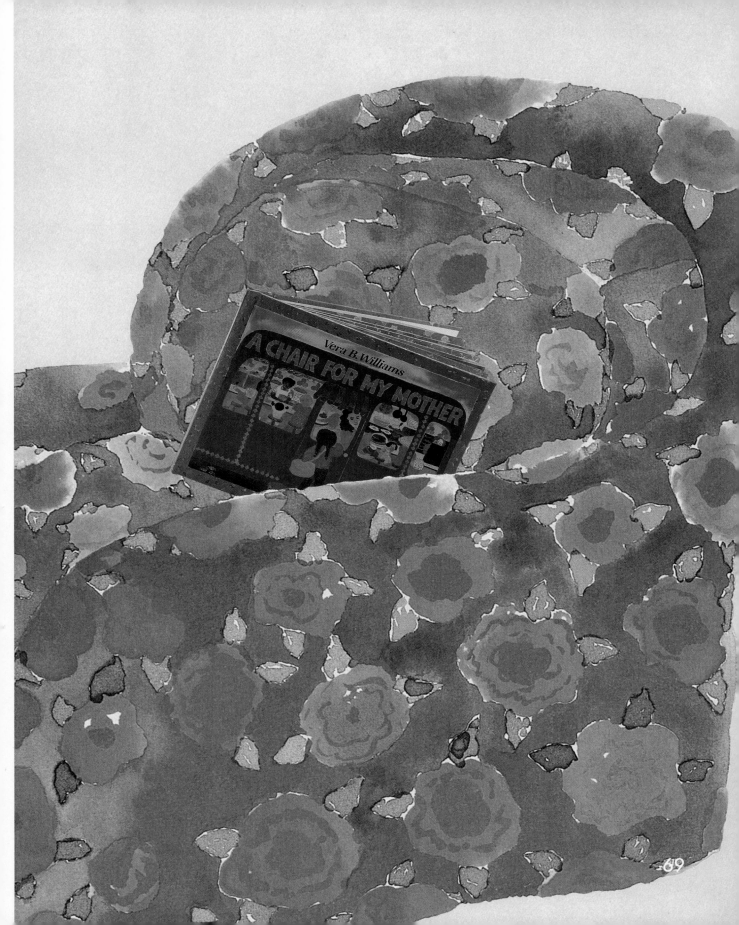

It takes a long time to fill a jar this big. Every day when my mother comes home from work, I take down the jar. My mama empties all her change from tips out of her purse for me to count. Then we push all of the coins into the jar.

Sometimes my mama is laughing when she comes home from work. Sometimes she's so tired she falls asleep while I count the money out into piles. Some days she has lots of tips. Some days she has only a little. Then she looks worried. But each evening every single shiny coin goes into the jar.

We sit in the kitchen to count the tips. Usually Grandma sits with us too. While we count, she likes to hum. Often she has money in her old leather wallet for us. Whenever she gets a good bargain on tomatoes or bananas or something she buys, she puts by the savings and they go into the jar.

When we can't get a single other coin into the jar, we are going to take out all the money and go and buy a chair.

Yes, a chair. A wonderful, beautiful, fat, soft armchair. We will get one covered in velvet with roses all over it. We are going to get the best chair in the whole world.

That is because our old chairs burned up. There was a big fire in our other house. All our chairs burned. So did our sofa and so did everything else. That wasn't such a long time ago.

My mother and I were coming home from buying new shoes. I had new sandals. She had new pumps. We were walking to our house from the bus. We were looking at everyone's tulips. She was saying she liked red tulips and I was saying I liked yellow ones. Then we came to our block.

Right outside our house stood two big fire engines. I could see lots of smoke. Tall orange flames came out of the roof. All the neighbors stood in a bunch across the street. Mama grabbed my hand and we ran. My uncle Sandy saw us and ran to us. Mama yelled, "Where's Mother?" I yelled, "Where's my grandma?" My aunt Ida waved and shouted, "She's here, she's here. She's O.K. Don't worry."

Grandma was all right. Our cat was safe too, though it took a while to find her. But everything else in our whole house was spoiled.

What was left of the house was turned to charcoal and ashes.

We went to stay with my mother's sister Aunt Ida and Uncle Sandy. Then we were able to move into the apartment downstairs. We painted the walls yellow. The floors were all shiny. But the rooms were very empty.

The first day we moved in, the neighbors brought pizza and cake and ice cream. And they brought a lot of other things too.

The family across the street brought a table and three kitchen chairs. The very old man next door gave us a bed from when his children were little.

My other grandpa brought us his beautiful rug. My mother's other sister, Sally, had made us red and

white curtains. Mama's boss, Josephine, brought
pots and pans, silverware and dishes. My cousin
brought me her own stuffed bear.

Everyone clapped when my grandma made a
speech. "You are all the kindest people," she said,
"and we thank you very, very much. It's lucky we're
young and can start all over."

That was last year, but we still have no sofa and no big chairs. When Mama comes home, her feet hurt. "There's no good place for me to take a load off my feet," she says. When Grandma wants to sit back and hum and cut up potatoes, she has to get as comfortable as she can on a hard kitchen chair.

So that is how come Mama brought home the biggest jar she could find at the diner and all the coins started to go into the jar.

Now the jar is too heavy for me to lift down. Uncle Sandy gave me a quarter. He had to boost me up so I could put it in.

After supper Mama and Grandma and I stood in front of the jar. "Well, I never would have believed it, but I guess it's full," Mama said.

My mother brought home little paper wrappers for the nickles and the dimes and the quarters. I counted them all out and wrapped them all up.

On my mother's day off, we took all the coins to the bank. The bank exchanged them for ten-dollar bills. Then we took the bus downtown to shop for our chair.

We shopped through four furniture stores. We tried out big chairs and smaller ones, high chairs and low chairs, soft chairs and harder ones. Grandma said she felt like Goldilocks in "The Three Bears" trying out all the chairs.

Finally we found the chair we were all dreaming of. And the money in the jar was enough to pay for it. We called Aunt Ida and Uncle Sandy. They came right down in their pickup truck to drive the chair home for us. They knew we couldn't wait for it to be delivered.

I tried out our chair in the back of the truck. Mama wouldn't let me sit there while we drove. But they let me sit in it while they carried it up to the door.

We set the chair right beside the window with the red and white curtains. Grandma and Mama and I all sat in it while Aunt Ida took our picture.

Now Grandma sits in it and talks with people going by in the daytime. Mama sits down and watches the news on TV when she comes home from her job. After supper, I sit with her and she can reach right up and turn out the light if I fall asleep in her lap.

Words FROM THE Author AND Illustrator

Dear Readers and Lookers,

I feel good that you are now acquainted with Rosa, her grandmother, and the rose-covered chair. Their story is printed here just as I wrote it but there is a lot of artwork from *A Chair for My Mother* that could not fit into this anthology.

I hope you will see the whole book sometime in a library or a bookstore or a classroom. I worked long and lovingly on every part of the book. It took almost a year to do—all the watercolored backgrounds behind the words, the borders, and the little extra pictures, everything right up to the pattern of roses on the back of the book jacket.

It was particularly important to me that everything come out just as vividly as I saw it with my inner eye. This was because I intended my book to be a special present. Yet I didn't realize this until I found myself creating the dedication page to my mother.

A Chair for My Mother was my way of saying goodbye to my mother after we were both grownup women and my mother died of an illness. But it was not only a private message. I was quite sure it grew out of feelings and experiences that a lot of readers shared with me. For instance, I remembered how tired my mother would be when she got home from a long day of work and sighed and pulled off her shoes. Even her shoes looked tired! We had to move often when I was a kid and I remembered how we tried to make each new apartment look beautiful even though we had very little.

Kids have pointed out to me that when you turn the first picture of the chair at an angle you see a heart shape. I didn't plan it that way. It probably came right out of my feeings. What to leave in and what to take out is an important part of a writer's and illustrator's work. But, to me, the most important part is to feel full of stories and pictures that I truly care about. Then I can work out how best to share them with you.

Vera B. Williams

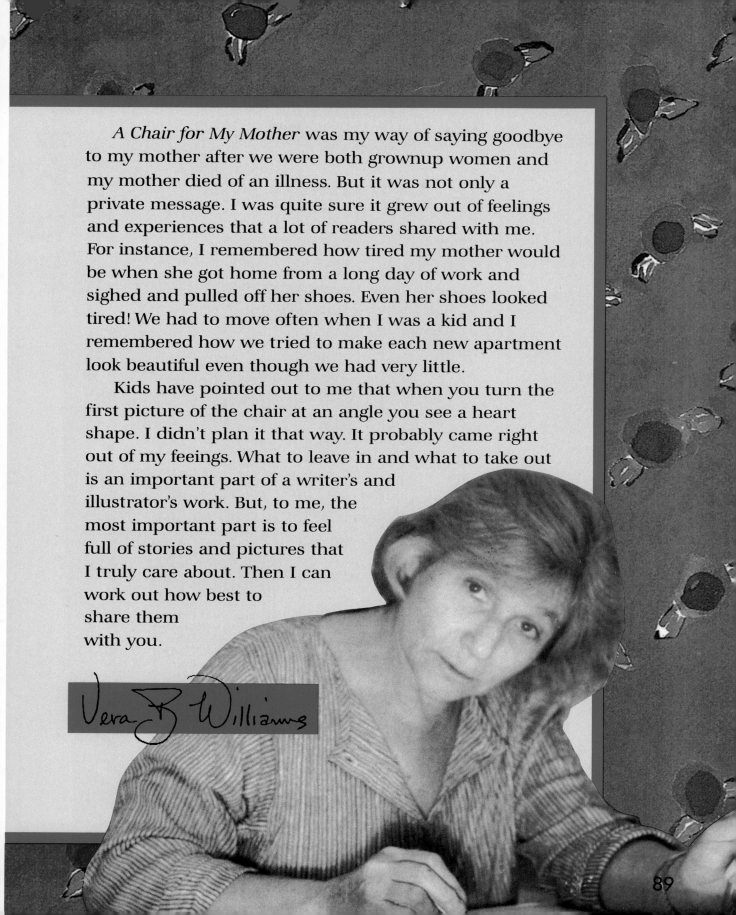

The Legend of the Indian Paintbrush

 retold and illustrated by
Tomie dePaola

Many years ago
when the People traveled the Plains
and lived in a circle of teepees,
there was a boy who was smaller
than the rest of the children in the tribe.
No matter how hard he tried,
he couldn't keep up with the other boys
who were always riding, running, shooting their bows,
and wrestling to prove their strength.
Sometimes his mother and father worried for him.

91

But the boy, who was called Little Gopher,
was not without a gift of his own.
From an early age, he made toy warriors
from scraps of leather and pieces of wood
and he loved to decorate smooth stones
with the red juices from berries
he found in the hills.
The wise shaman of the tribe understood
that Little Gopher had a gift that was special.
"Do not struggle, Little Gopher.
Your path will not be the same as the others.
They will grow up to be warriors.
Your place among the People will be remembered
for a different reason."

And in a few years
when Little Gopher was older,
he went out to the hills alone
to think about becoming a man,
for this was the custom of the tribe.
And it was there that a Dream-Vision came to him.

The sky filled with clouds and out of them
came a young Indian maiden and an old grandfather.
She carried a rolled-up animal skin
and he carried a brush made of fine animal hairs
and pots of paints.

The grandfather spoke.
"My son, these are the tools
by which you shall become great among your People.
You will paint pictures of the deeds of the warriors
and the visions of the shaman,
and the People shall see them and remember them forever."

The maiden unrolled a pure white buckskin
and placed it on the ground.
"Find a buckskin as white as this," she told him.
"Keep it and one day you will paint a picture
that is as pure as the colors
in the evening sky."

And as she finished speaking, the clouds cleared
and a sunset of great beauty filled the sky.
Little Gopher looked at the white buckskin
and on it he saw colors as bright and beautiful
as those made by the setting sun.

Then the sun slowly sank behind the hills,
the sky grew dark,
and the Dream-Vision was over.
Little Gopher returned to the circle of the People.

The next day he began to make soft brushes
from the hairs of different animals
and stiff brushes from the hair of the horses' tails.
He gathered berries and flowers
and rocks of different colors
and crushed them to make his paints.

He collected the skins of animals,
which the warriors brought home from their hunts.
He stretched the skins on wooden frames
and pulled them until they were tight.

And he began to paint pictures . . .

Of great hunts . . .

Of great deeds . . .

Of great Dream-Visions . . .
So that the People would always remember.

But even as he painted,
Little Gopher sometimes longed
to put aside his brushes
and ride out with the warriors.
But always he remembered his Dream-Vision
and he did not go with them.

Many months ago,
he had found his pure white buckskin,
but it remained empty
because he could not find the colors of the sunset.
He used the brightest flowers,
the reddest berries,
and the deepest purples from the rocks,
and still his paintings never satisfied him.
They looked dull and dark.

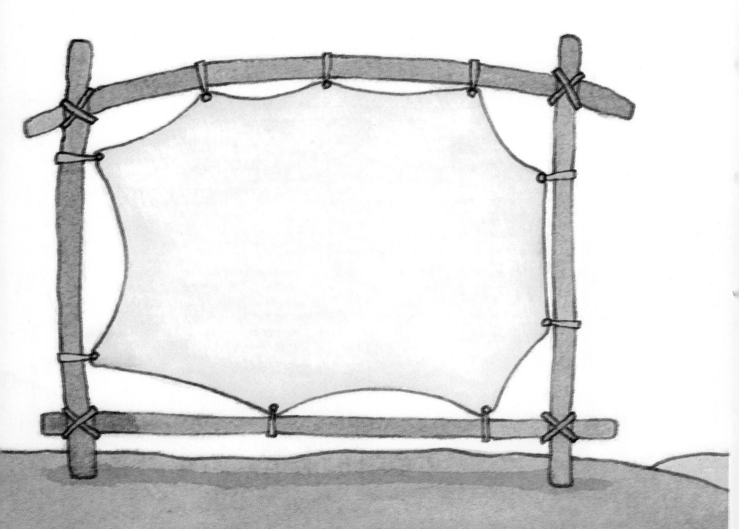

He began to go to the top of a hill each evening
and look at the colors that filled the sky
to try and understand how to make them.
He longed to share the beauty of his Dream-Vision
with the People.

But he never gave up trying,
and every morning when he awoke
he took out his brushes and his pots of paints
and created the stories of the People
with the tools he had.

One night as he lay awake,
he heard a voice calling to him.
"Because you have been faithful to the People
and true to your gift,
you shall find the colors you are seeking.
Tomorrow take the white buckskin
and go to the place
where you watch the sun in the evening.
There on the ground you will find what you need."

The next evening as the sun began to go down,
Little Gopher put aside his brushes
and went to the top of the hill
as the colors of the sunset spread across the sky.

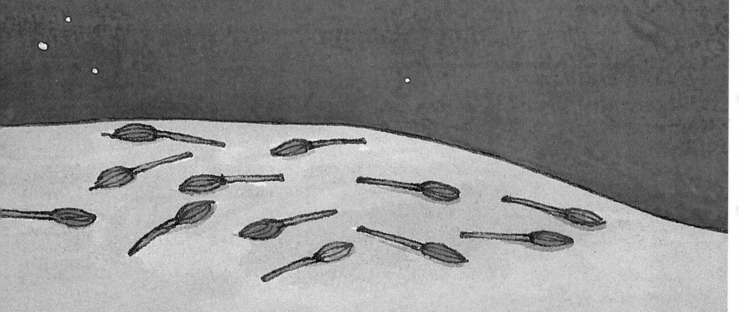

And there, on the ground all around him,
were brushes filled with paint,
each one a color of the sunset.
Little Gopher began to paint quickly and surely,
using one brush, then another.

And as the colors in the sky began to fade,
Little Gopher gazed at the white buckskin
and he was happy.

He had found the colors of the sunset.
He carried his painting down
to the circle of the People,
leaving the brushes on the hillside.

And the next day, when the People awoke,
the hill was ablaze with color,
for the brushes had taken root in the earth
and multiplied into plants
of brilliant reds, oranges and yellows.

And every spring from that time,
the hills and meadows burst into bloom.

And every spring,
the People danced and sang the praises
of Little Gopher who had painted for the People.

And the People no longer called him Little Gopher,
but He-Who-Brought-the-Sunset-to-the-Earth.

a Note from the Author:

Tomie dePaola

The lovely red, orange, yellow (and even pink) Indian Paintbrush blooms in Wyoming, Texas, and the high plains, and has many stories connected with its origin. The story of the Native American artist and his desire to paint the sunset was meaningful to me as an artist. (There are many times when I wish I could go out on a hill and find brushes filled with exactly the colors I need.)

The idea for doing a book on this wildflower came from my good friend Pat Henry after she had seen my book *The Legend of the Bluebonnet*, which is the story of the Texas state flower. Pat is from Wyoming where the Indian Paintbrush is the state flower.

Carolyn Sullivan from Austin, Texas, had recently sent me a copy of *Texas Wildflowers, Stories and Legends*. Carolyn is a teacher in the Austin area, and in 1965 this collection was made available to teachers there for use with a unit on Texas trees and wildflowers. She too had read the bluebonnet book and knew of my interest in folktale and legend. The Indian Paintbrush is a familiar flower to Texans and in the book I came across a brief and interesting account of how the wildflower got its name.

STERLING

The Rescue of a Baby Harbor Seal

by Sandra Verrill White
and Michael Filisky

AWARD-WINNING AUTHORS

In the cold ocean off the coast of New England, an animal has come to the surface. What kind of animal is it? It is a seal. In fact, it is the most common kind of seal found in New England. It is a harbor seal.

Harbor seals are different from other northern seals. Gray seals like this fuzzy pup have much longer, horselike faces.

Hooded seals are much larger than harbor seals. Hooded seal pups have a beautiful dark back and cream-colored belly.

Harp seals, which are dark as adults, give birth to snow-white pups.

But only the harbor seals live in New England in large numbers. Several thousand of them make their homes off the coast of Maine.

A harbor seal hunts in the water and rests on the rocks by the shore. Its earholes and nostrils close tight to keep out icy waters; its large eyes and sensitive whiskers help it search the rocks for signs of food.

The harbor seal shares its underwater habitat with many kinds of animals and plants. Dense mats of rockweeds sway in the current. Periwinkle snails and prickly sea urchins graze on the seaweeds, while starfish search for tasty mussels. None of these tempt harbor seals.

Schools of small, silvery fish swim among the rocks and seaweeds. Usually, harbor seals try to catch slower-swimming fish than these.

A seal decides to come out of the water. Carefully, it hauls itself out onto the rocks that have been exposed by the outgoing tide.

This seal is a female, heavy with her first pup. She has come out of the water to give birth.

Away from other seals, the new pup comes into the world. Mother and pup touch noses and call to each other, learning each other's smells and sounds. Briefly, the pup nurses on her mother's rich milk and sleeps by her side.

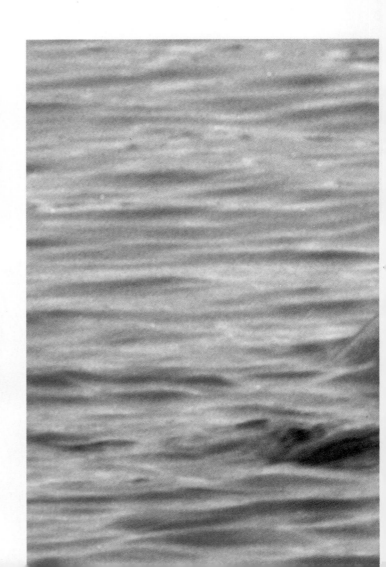

After several hours alone, the pup becomes hungry. She looks expectantly toward the sea, but there is no sign of her mother. Soon the harbor seal pup becomes distressed and calls softly.

By morning the pup is frantic for food.

Several days later the mother seal has still not appeared. Dazed and weak, the pup wanders from the rocks to the beach.

Every spring on the coast of New England people find baby seals. Some of the pups have been orphaned, but most mother seals have just gone on short fishing trips. Fortunately, people also find signs like this one.

The newborn follows her mother into the ocean. Newborn harbor seal pups have little insulating fat, so they cannot stay long in the chilly water. The pup returns to the beach to wait in the sun while her mother feeds in the sea. In a few days the pup's bright red birth cord will dry and fall off.

Someone from the Marine Mammal Stranding Network must determine that the little seal has really been abandoned.

The Marine Mammal Stranding coordinator sees how thin the pup is and knows this means the pup is probably a real orphan. The pup is immediately brought to the Animal Care Facility at the New England Aquarium.

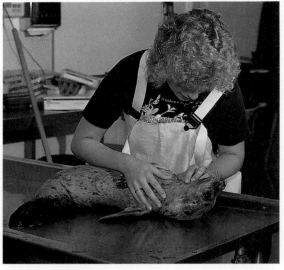

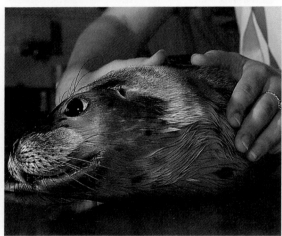

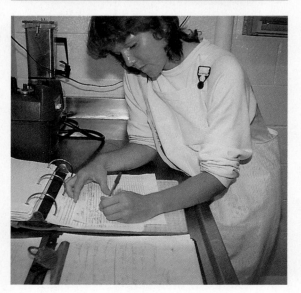

At the New England Aquarium the pup is placed on a steel examining table in a clean, bright room. Animal-care specialists check her temperature, weigh her, test her reflexes, and note her activity. The pup watches but is too weak to move.

Everything about the harbor seal pup is recorded on her own chart. To identify her, a temporary tag is glued to the hair on her head. Every orphaned pup is given a name. Like most pups, she lost her very pale newborn coat a few days after birth. But because she still has a silvery sheen to her fur, she is called Sterling.

Sterling is placed in the holding area, where other pups snooze under the warm lamps. She nuzzles up to them and falls asleep.

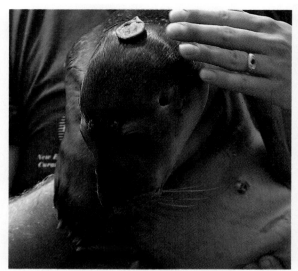

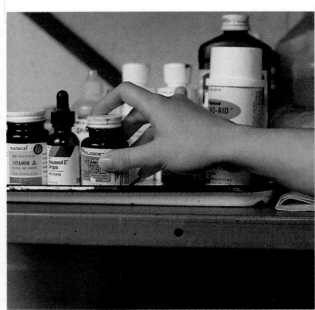
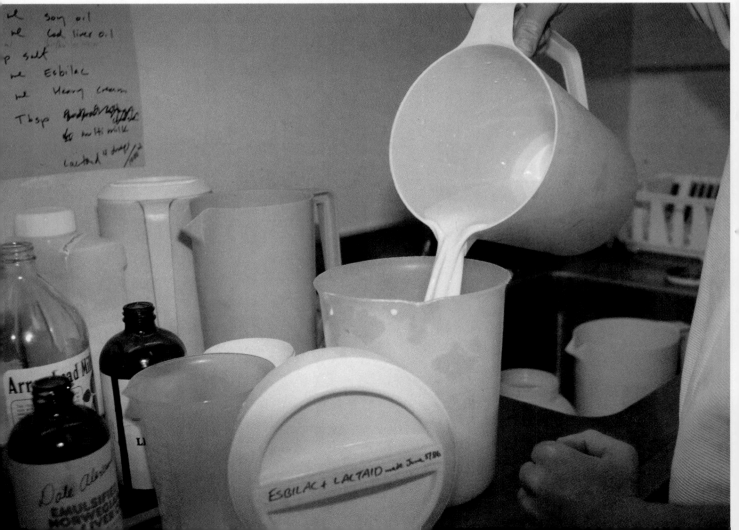

Waking up, Sterling hears the voices of the keepers as they prepare infant seal formula. Making formula is messy work. Pounds of herring are filleted, then pureed in a blender. This fish mush is added to heavy cream, vegetable oil, vitamins, and minerals until it is the consistency of a thin milk shake. A portion is measured out for each pup and warmed before feeding.

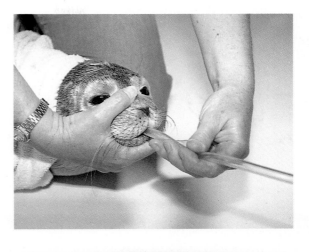

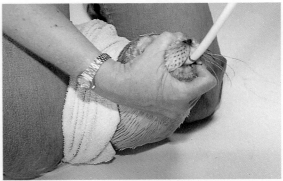

Sterling is so thin that the keepers are very worried. If they can't get plenty of the nourishing formula into her stomach, Sterling will not live long. Sick seal pups find it difficult to nurse from a bottle. To feed Sterling, a flexible tube is inserted into her mouth and gently guided into her stomach. In only minutes her stomach is full.

After the feedings, the keepers make notes about each pup and clean the pen with antiseptics. Their hunger satisfied, the pups sleep contentedly.

Later in the day, most of the pups follow the keepers around, begging for food and attention. Exercise is important for recovering seal pups, but when Sterling is introduced to the seal pup "swimming pool," she is too weak to play or swim. She flops out and wriggles onto a keeper's lap.

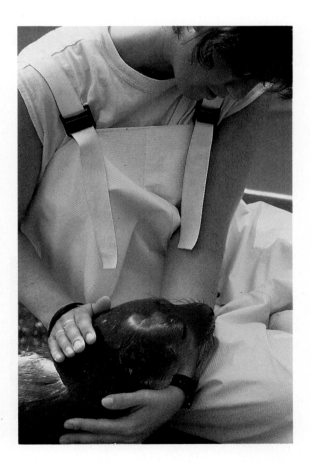

In several weeks, Sterling has put on weight and grown teeth. If the keepers aren't careful, they can get nipped. After all, Sterling is still a wild harbor seal.

As the pups get stronger, they become more independent of the keepers. The little seals sleep and play together as a group. A daily swim helps prepare them for life in the ocean.

One day the keepers place some thawed fish in the pool to interest the pups in solid food. The pups nudge the fish around, biting at them. They are great playthings.

The seal pups play with the fish for several days. Then, one afternoon the pups are especially hungry. Sterling takes a fish into the water. She holds it briefly in her mouth and then swallows it whole. Sterling has "caught" her first meal.

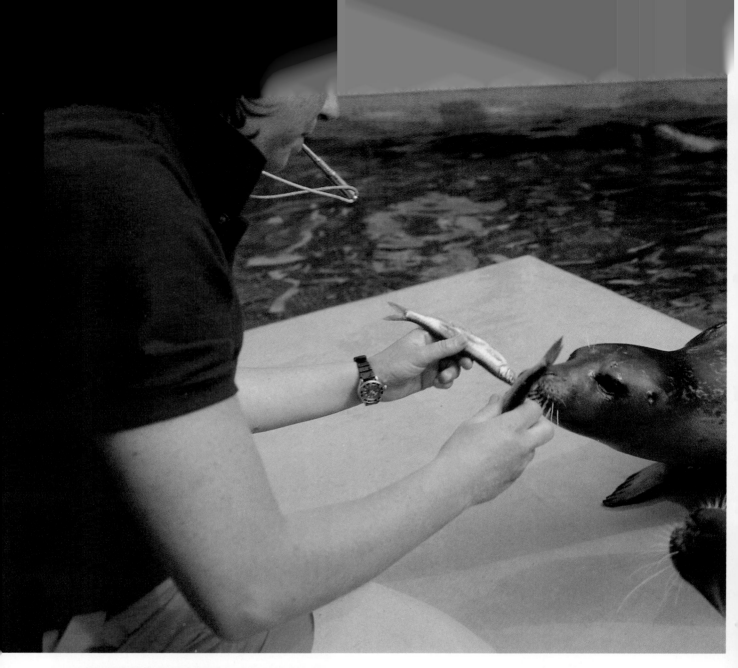

It doesn't take the other pups long to catch on to feeding and, when they learn how to eat fish, it seems they enjoy eating better than anything.

After two months, most of the pups have tripled their birth weight. They are swimming and eating just like adults. The time has come for their release into the wild.

Two pups are ready for release. One of them is Sterling. They are taken by van to the coast of Maine, where a colony of harbor seals has been spotted.

When the cages are opened Sterling dashes right into the water. The other pup is timid and carefully slides into the waves. In a few days the seals will lose their tags in the water.

Eventually both pups are so far away the keepers can't tell them apart from the wild seals. The rescued orphans are on their own.

There are many dangers in the sea for a young harbor seal. Sharks and other predators are always a threat. In recent years, however, dangers made by man have become very serious: chemical pollution, crowded harbors, garbage dumped in the sea.

People can cause problems for seals, but people can help, too. At the New England Aquarium, the Marine Mammal Stranding Network learns important facts about wild seals and their rehabilitation. This kind of knowledge could someday help save endangered seal species, such as the Hawaiian monk seal. The rescue of Sterling and the other baby harbor seals helps ensure there will always be wild animals in the waters of the world.

ALA NOTABLE BOOK

CHILDREN'S CHOICE

TEACHERS' CHOICE

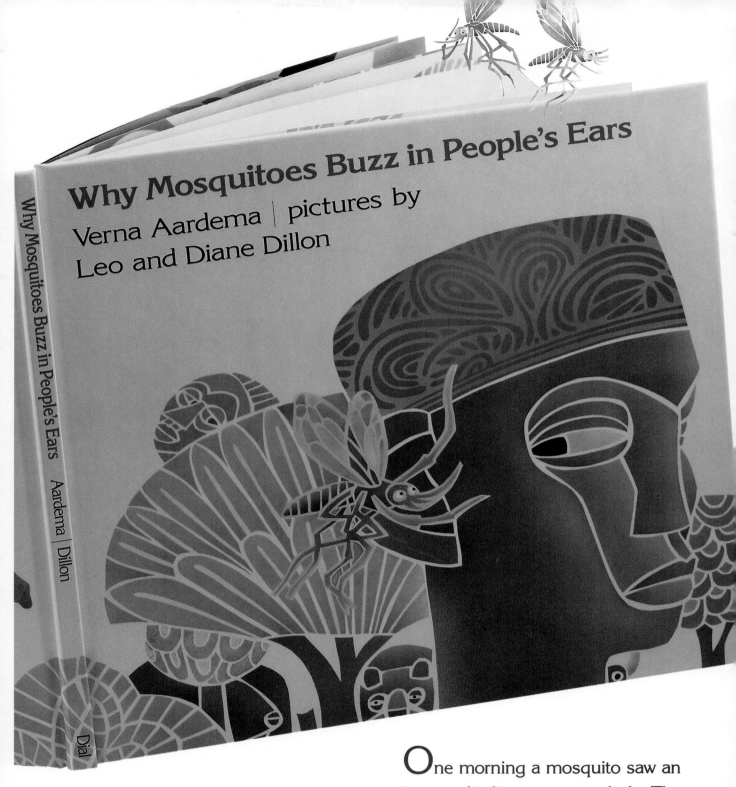

Why Mosquitoes Buzz in People's Ears

Verna Aardema | pictures by
Leo and Diane Dillon

One morning a mosquito saw an iguana drinking at a waterhole. The mosquito said, "Iguana, you will never believe what I saw yesterday."

149

"Try me," said the iguana.

The mosquito said, "I saw a farmer digging yams that were almost as big as I am."

"What's a mosquito compared to a yam?" snapped
the iguana grumpily. "I would rather be deaf than listen
to such nonsense!" Then he stuck two sticks in his ears
and went off, mek, mek, mek, mek, through the reeds.

The iguana was still grumbling to himself when he happened to pass by a python.

The big snake raised his head and said, "Good morning, Iguana."

The iguana did not answer but lumbered on, bobbing his head, badamin, badamin.

"Now, why won't he speak to me?" said the python to himself. "Iguana must be angry about something. I'm

afraid he is plotting some mischief against me!" He
began looking for somewhere to hide. The first likely
place he found was a rabbit hole, and in it he went,
wasawusu, wasawusu, wasawusu.

When the rabbit saw the big snake coming into her
burrow, she was terrified. She scurried out through her
back way and bounded, krik, krik, krik, across a clearing.

A crow saw the rabbit running for her life. He flew into the forest crying kaa, kaa, kaa! It was his duty to spread the alarm in case of danger.

A monkey heard the crow. He was sure that some dangerous beast was prowling near. He began screeching and leaping kili wili through the trees to help warn the other animals.

As the monkey was crashing through the treetops, he happened to land on a dead limb. It broke and fell on an owl's nest, killing one of the owlets.

Mother Owl was not at home. For though she usually
hunted only in the night, this morning she was still out
searching for one more tidbit to satisfy her hungry
babies. When she returned to the nest, she found one of
them dead. Her other children told her that the monkey
had killed it. All that day and all that night, she sat in her
tree—so sad, so sad, so sad!

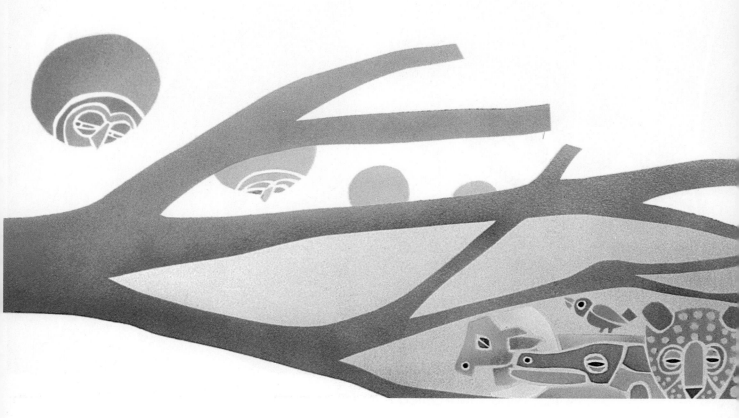

Now it was Mother Owl who woke the sun each day
so that the dawn could come. But this time, when she
should have hooted for the sun, she did not do it.

The night grew longer and longer. The animals of the
forest knew it was lasting much too long. They feared
that the sun would never come back.

At last King Lion called a meeting of the animals. They came and sat down, pem, pem, pem, around a council fire. Mother Owl did not come, so the antelope was sent to fetch her.

When she arrived, King Lion asked, "Mother Owl, why have you not called the sun? The night has lasted long, long, long, and everyone is worried."

Mother Owl said, "Monkey killed one of my owlets.
Because of that, I cannot bear to wake the sun."

The king said to the gathered animals:

"Did you hear?

It was the monkey

who killed the owlet—

and now Mother Owl won't wake the sun

so that the day can come."

Then King Lion called the monkey. He came
before him nervously glancing from side to side, rim,
rim, rim, rim.

"Monkey," said the king, "why did you kill one of
Mother Owl's babies?"

"Oh, King," said the monkey, "it was the crow's fault.
He was calling and calling to warn us of danger. And I
went leaping through the trees to help. A limb broke
under me, and it fell taaa on the owl's nest."

The king said to the council:
"So, it was the crow
who alarmed the monkey,
who killed the owlet—
and now Mother Owl won't wake the sun
so that the day can come."

Then the king called for the crow. That big bird came flapping up. He said, "King Lion, it was the rabbit's fault! I saw her running for her life in the daytime. Wasn't that reason enough to spread an alarm?"

The king nodded his head and said to the council:
"So, it was the rabbit
who startled the crow,
who alarmed the monkey,
who killed the owlet—
and now Mother Owl won't wake the sun
so that the day can come."

Then King Lion called the rabbit. The timid little creature stood before him, one trembling paw drawn up uncertainly.

"Rabbit," cried the king, "why did you break a law of nature and go running, running, running, in the daytime?"

"Oh, King," said the rabbit, "it was the python's fault. I was in my house minding my own business when that big snake came in and chased me out."

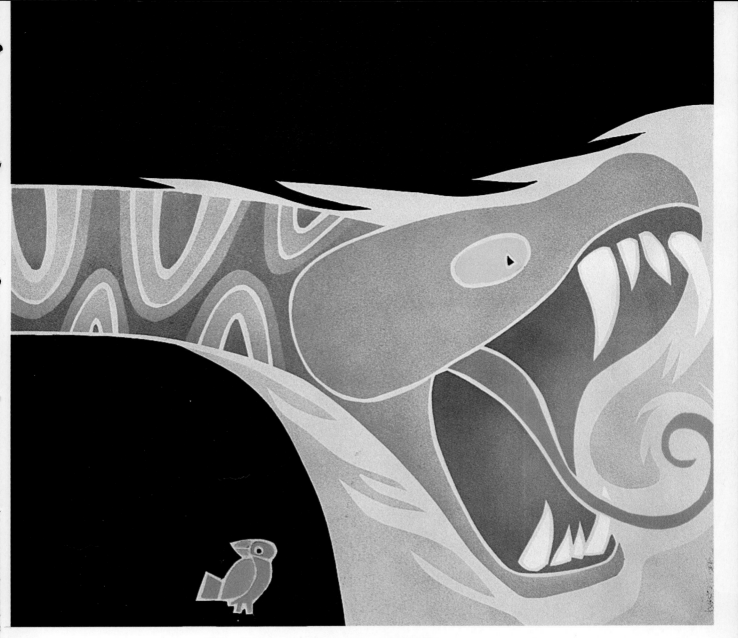

The king said to the council:
"So, it was the python
who scared the rabbit,
who startled the crow,
who alarmed the monkey,
who killed the owlet—
and now Mother Owl won't wake the sun
so that the day can come."

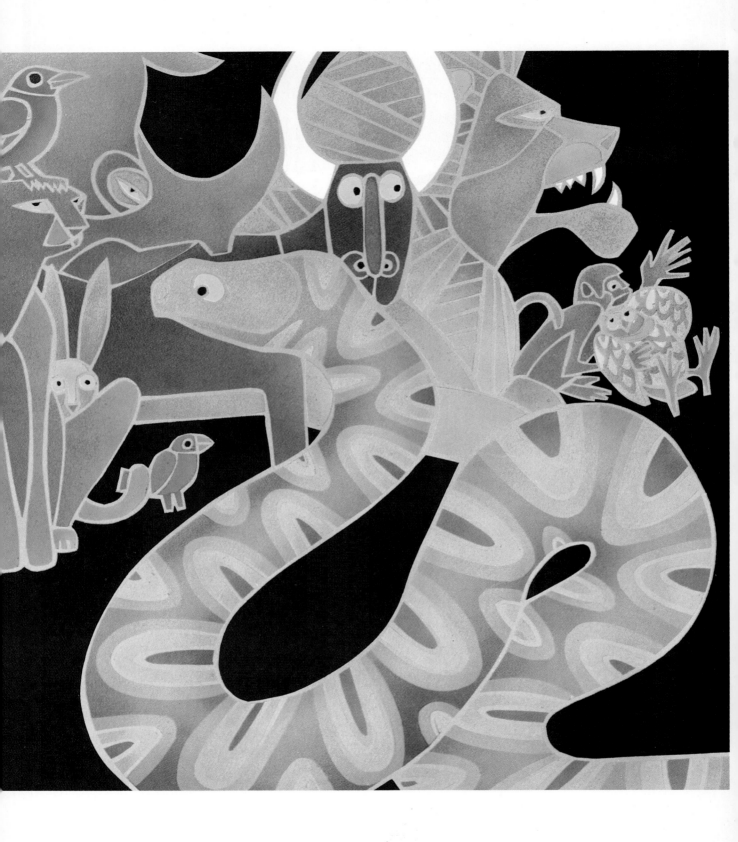

King Lion called the python, who came slithering, wasawusu, wasawusu, past the other animals. "But, King," he cried, "it was the iguana's fault! He wouldn't speak to me. And I thought he was plotting some mischief against me. When I crawled into the rabbit's hole, I was only trying to hide."

The king said to the council:

"So, it was the iguana

who frightened the python,

who scared the rabbit,

who startled the crow,

who alarmed the monkey,

who killed the owlet—

and now Mother Owl won't wake the sun

so that the day can come."

Now the iguana was not at the meeting. For he had not heard the summons.

The antelope was sent to fetch him.

All the animals laughed when they saw the iguana coming, badamin, badamin, with the sticks still stuck in his ears!

King Lion pulled out the sticks, purup, purup. Then he asked, "Iguana, what evil have you been plotting against the python?"

"None! None at all!" cried the iguana. "Python is my friend!"

"Then why wouldn't you say good morning to me?" demanded the snake.

"I didn't hear you, or even see you!" said the iguana. "Mosquito told me such a big lie, I couldn't bear to listen to it. So I put sticks in my ears."

"Nge, nge, nge," laughed the lion. "So that's why you had sticks in your ears!"

"Yes," said the iguana. "It was the mosquito's fault."

King Lion said to the council:

"So, it was the mosquito
who annoyed the iguana,
who frightened the python,
who scared the rabbit,
who startled the crow,
who alarmed the monkey,
who killed the owlet—
and now Mother Owl won't wake the sun
so that the day can come."

"Punish the mosquito! Punish the mosquito!" cried all the animals.

When Mother Owl heard that, she was satisfied. She turned her head toward the east and hooted: "Hoo! Hooooo! Hooooooo!"

And the sun came up.

Meanwhile the mosquito had listened to it all from a nearby bush. She crept under a curly leaf, *semm*, and was never found and brought before the council.

But because of this the mosquito has a guilty conscience. To this day she goes about whining in people's ears: "Zeee! Is everyone still angry at me?"

When she does that, she gets an honest answer.

KPAO!

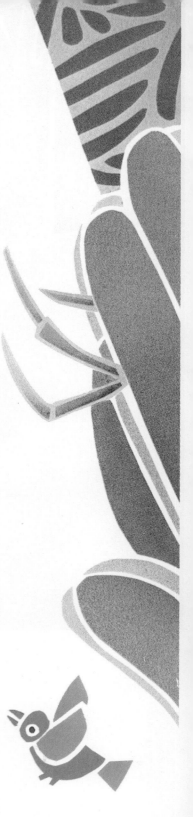

WORDS FROM THE ILLUSTRATORS:

LEO AND DIANE DILLON

Sometimes people ask how the two of us work together as artists. First, one or both of us read the manuscript for the book that is to be illustrated. Then we decide how we want the pictures to look—what style to use and which techniques. Sometimes that takes days and days! One of us will throw out an idea and the other won't be too excited about it. After much give and take, we decide what kind of pictures will work best for the story.

One question people often ask about artists working together is *Who holds the brush?* Actually, we both do. One of us starts starts the drawing and gives it to the other at some point. Individually, our styles are very different. If each of us worked alone on a page, all the pages would look different even though we had agreed on the way to draw them. Together, we create a third style that is *our* style.

We first started working together thirty-four years ago. We decided that if we were going to be married, we would have to work on the same projects. We had been competitors in school, and we didn't like that. Now our son is becoming a painter, and though he has helped us with some of our books, he wants to paint pictures that will hang in an art gallery.

We were asked by the book publisher to do the pictures for *Why Mosquitoes Buzz in People's Ears*. It was one of the first picture books that we did. It was a chance to do big, bold pictures that we thought children would like. The nice thing about that story is that it is full of images. There is so much going on in the story, we had lots of choices about what to illustrate.

Our advice to children who want to draw is to draw constantly. In doing that, you are exercising the strength in your hand, in your eyes, and in your mind. Looking at life around you is very important. That's where you'll get your ideas for images. Artistic talent isn't just something that you are born with, something that will flow out of your fingers. You need to work at it. Then, when you look back, you'll see how much you've improved.

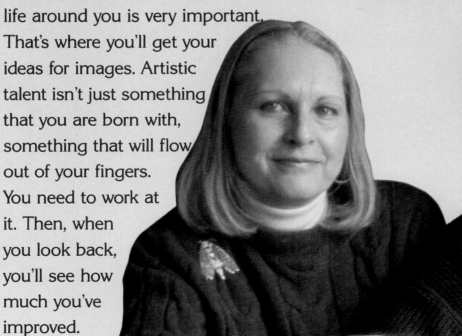

The Great Fishing Contest

The Great Fishing Contest

BY DAVID KHERDIAN
ILLUSTRATED BY
NONNY HOGROGIAN

AWARD-WINNING AUTHOR

ONE

"School's out" means something different to everybody.
To me and Sammy it means three more weeks until
The Great Fishing Contest. That's our name for it. I'm
not sure it has an official name, unless it's something
like "the fishing contest at the zoo pond for children
under twelve on July 3rd from 12 noon to 2 P.M."

But that doesn't begin to get into the details, and
details are what everything is about.

For one thing, the first prize is a complete spinning outfit. That's the first and most important detail. That's the best part of the contest, but in another way it's the worst. Because if I win the first prize it means that Sammy won't. And if Sammy wins, I don't. Either way, this would be enough to spoil the contest for *both* of us, and that's why we had to put our heads together right at the beginning and figure out what we would do if one of us actually *got* the first prize.

"If that happens," I announced one day as we were walking home from school, "we'll get odd jobs until we've made enough money for the other guy to buy a similar outfit."

"Let's shake on it, Jason," Sammy said.

And that's what we did, but not before spitting on our palms for good luck.

The day after school let out we walked to the zoo in order to check out the pond. This was probably the 132nd time we'd checked out the pond since we first entered the contest, but that didn't make it any less exciting for either of us. We both knew it was a shallow pond used mainly by young kids for sailing boats, by older kids for skating, and by ducks and geese for wading in and swimming.

"It's a pretty usual pond," Sammy said, as we stood on the bank surveying all of it at a glance.

"Except for one thing," I said, "the footbridge that divides this pond from the fenced-in one that's off-limits."

"Doesn't matter," Sammy answered. "You can't fish from the bridge."

"And you can't fish from the banks because they're too steep."

"And you can't go in the water, and if you *fall* in you're disqualified."

We had walked over to the middle of the footbridge and were staring down at the water beneath it.

"It's so deep here you can't see the bottom," Sammy said.

"What does that mean?"

"It means the biggest fish are probably down there."

"Not necessarily," I said. "There's a screen that divides the two ponds." I could tell Sammy didn't know what I was talking about.

We gave that detail some thought as we turned and walked to the opposite railing and looked out over the pond that was off-limits. This was the pond where the ducks and geese and other birds went when they didn't want to be bothered, like when they were having babies. The fence around the pond wasn't meant to keep them in but to keep us out.

"Do you think those older guys we heard about really took those fourteen-inch bluegills out of there last summer?"

"I don't know, Jason. What do you think?"

I looked out over the off-limits pond and gave it some thought. "It's deep enough," I answered. "It's plenty deep enough to hold some big fish."

"I wouldn't be daring enough to sneak in at night, would you? Even if I could scale that fence."

"I'd give almost anything to catch a fourteen-inch bluegill," I said, avoiding a straight answer.

We turned around and went back to the other railing. "A fourteen-inch bluegill would practically have to swim with his fins out of the water on this side," Sammy announced, as we surveyed the main pond again.

"That's right!" I exclaimed, and all at once I visualized the pond in winter, with the skaters carefully maneuvering between the fins of these huge bluegills that had gotten themselves frozen into place.

"What are you thinking, Jason?"

"Did it ever occur to you, Sammy, that this pond freezes solid in the winter?"

"Sure—but so what?"

"Well, there are always enough fish for the contest in the summer, so if the pond freezes solid in the winter, where do they come from? Fish aren't planted, you know."

Sammy gave a start, and then jerked his thumb over his shoulder toward the other pond. "Over there!"

"That's right, which means that the screen under the bridge doesn't go all the way to the bottom, so it keeps people from sneaking into that part of the pond but doesn't keep the fish out of *this* part."

"Remember when we came out here during spring vacation and saw the bluegills with their spawning nests along the bank in the main pond?"

"All smoothed out, with the hollow in the center where the eggs must have been."

"Right! So where do you think those mother bluegills came from?"

"In there," Sammy answered, pointing over his shoulder again. "And I guess that's why the baby bluegills stay *here*, because if they went back in *there* they'd be eaten by those lunkers."

"I guess the ones that survive the fishing contest are big enough to go back to the off-limits pond by wintertime. And it means there are plenty more where they came from."

"It's quite a system, isn't it?"

"Yeah, and mostly invisible."

TWO

I don't know if we had made any headway in our planning for the fishing contest, but we both felt like we had made some discoveries. And we definitely had something to think about.

The reason we were so eager to win the spinning rod was because my dad always said that when we got old enough he'd take us fishing on one of the big lakes outside of town. And old enough to us meant having our own spinning rods, with tackle boxes to match. Sammy and I couldn't afford either one, and since Sammy's parents were divorced, with his dad living in another town, I wasn't going to ask my dad for something—even something I was pretty sure he'd never buy for me—if it meant Sammy couldn't have one too.

The idea was to win that spinning rod, because then my dad would see that we were ready for fishing out of a boat for game fish, and not just pan fish, which was all we were able to do now.

Actually, if the river that ran through our town hadn't been polluted, we probably would have been satisfied to fish there. Once upon a time it had black bass and pickerel, and then later you could still catch rock bass, bluegills and bullheads, but now the only things left are carp and suckers, and it's dangerous to eat them. Sammy and I feel the same way: you shouldn't catch what you don't intend to eat.

The only time we go fishing now is when we hike out to this small lake on the outskirts of town. It's so shallow along the banks, and so crowded with trees, that the only way you can catch any fish is to get out in the middle, where it's still pretty shallow. We have this flotation tube that Sammy got one Christmas that we pump up once we get to the lake, and it's just big enough for the two of us. We have to use very short poles or else we get all tangled up. One time we brought long poles. We floated around the lake, hollering at each other, getting tangled, and arguing about whose turn it was to paddle; it made it impossible to get really serious about fishing. About the only thing that kept us on the job was the promise of a fish fry afterward.

We always bring a couple of potatoes along, plus a little griddle, and of course salt and pepper. We bury the potatoes in the coals of the fire and cook the fish on the griddle, but only after we've done our preparatory work. We have this secret place where we do our cooking that we keep camouflaged, and so far no one's discovered it.

Since two potatoes aren't enough for an outdoor lunch, we *have* to catch fish, and so far we always have, although one time we caught only two small crappies, and there was more ceremony than food to our "outdoor repast" that day. *Repast* is one of those words we picked up from reading the outdoor fishing and hunting magazines, which we do a lot of. We've figured out that the less you do of something the more time you have to spend reading about it, and dreaming about it.

But we'd rather read about fishing than collect baseball cards and dream about being Big Leaguers. We both like exploring and discovering things. Collecting is okay but it takes money, and no matter how much you have of something you always want more. That's especially true of baseball cards. Ask anyone who collects them.

Collecting and adventuring are very definitely two different things.

THREE

"We have to decide if it's good luck to try and earn enough money for one spinning rod before the fishing contest. That way if one of us wins the first prize we'll both have a rod." We were having a serious conference in my bedroom, which is where we always go when we have a "major decision" to make. It's the only place we can go where we know we won't be overheard, and my mom's been given strict instructions not to interrupt us unless it's something important, like something she's just baked. Cookies, for instance.

We both went silent and set to thinking. Luck was a detail you couldn't forget, but it was one of the hardest to figure out.

"It could be good luck, and then it could be bad," Sammy answered. "We have to decide."

"Can we get some help with our decision?"

"For instance?"

"My sister opens this book called the *I Ching*, and then she throws a couple of coins, which tell her what to do next."

"How does it work?"

"Beats me."

"Let's not try it, then. Any other ideas?"

"Maybe we can try a little reason instead. If we already have enough money for one rod, maybe luck won't be on our side for the contest."

"Like we're being greedy."

"It could be that wanting too much brings bad luck."

"It wouldn't make sense that greed could bring *good* luck."

"I think you're right, it doesn't figure."

"There's another thing, if one of us wins first prize, that might mean we're lucky, and then getting the second rod will be easier because we'll have luck on our side."

"That's right, and it will mean that our luck didn't come from greed. It came from something else."

"It might be best not to know what that other thing is, just in case knowing puts a jinx on it."

"I should have thought of that myself," I said. "It's perfect!"

My mom had to knock twice before we heard her and told her it was okay to come in. Instead of jumping up for the cookies and milk that she was bringing in—like we usually do—we told her to put the tray on the bureau. She looked at us kind of funny but didn't say anything until she got to the door. "A couple of deep thinkers," she mumbled as she closed the door behind her.

FOUR

"Corks are best," Sammy was saying. We were sitting on his front steps watching the sun go down. There were only two days left until the contest. "With a cork you always know what the fish is doing when it bites. And we both know just when to set the hook, which is more than you can say for most of the kids who go to the contest."

"If you use a cork you can't get the line out as far."

"But with all the small fish around, if you don't use a cork you can lose your bait and not even know you had a bite."

"You have to use a tiny cork and be sure not to put any sinkers on the line. That way they can run more easily with the bait."

"The real question is how to catch the biggest fish. All the other prizes are based on the total weight of all the fish caught, but we want the first prize."

"But since catching the biggest fish is mainly luck, shouldn't we catch as many as we can? That way we're working on the law of averages."

"The law of averages is okay but it's kind of sloppy. Not very scientific, if you ask me."

"If you ask me, the trouble with this contest is that it's too much chance and not enough skill."

"But that's just what I was trying to say. I don't think we're on the same wavelength today, Sammy."

We were silent for a while, mainly because the sun was big, and red, and glorious, and would soon be out of sight.

"I always figure there's a secret to everything," I said. "Knowing how to catch a fish is one thing, but I still say the secret is knowing *where* they are. In this case, where the biggest fish is, or is apt to be."

"I think you're getting over your head. The contest is always won by an eight- or nine-inch fish, and the biggest fish is never more than a half-inch larger than the second biggest fish. Seems to me it's pure luck. Being in the right place at the right time with the right bait. Period."

"But what if that isn't the case?"

The sun had disappeared and put an end to our argument.

FIVE

It was the day before The Great Fishing Contest. All the other kids were out buying firecrackers and sparklers and all the other junk that goes with the Fourth of July. We hadn't exactly outgrown our love of firecrackers, but they weren't included in our pact to save all the money we could for fishing and exploring.

We were going over the rules one last time. We each had a regulation five-foot pole—any poles longer than that would have resulted in endless tangles and mixed lines. Also you couldn't fish so close that you touched the person next to you. Everyone was allowed to bring a bucket, which could include a can or container for bait because everyone fished with worms. As for extra lines and hooks and bobbers, they had to be carried "on the person."

Most of the contestants didn't bother with bringing extra equipment, but that was not the way with Sammy and me. "We have to be prepared for every eventuality," was how Sammy summed it up. We each had an extra cork, in which we imbedded two hooks. We also carried extra line.

The other rule was that you couldn't change places once the starting flag waved.

And we couldn't forget the most important rule of all: Time. The contest lasted from twelve to two, but you could show up for the contest anytime that day you wanted. Sammy and I planned to get there at least one hour ahead. Everyone said it didn't matter where you fished because the pond was the same from one end to the other, but everyone knew each spot where the winning fish had been taken since the contest began in 1981, and each person, I suppose, had his own idea of which of those spots was the best.

On this score Sammy had something to say that was pretty smart. "Have you noticed there haven't been any repeats? For that reason alone a guy would be better off going to a different spot than one that's already won."

"You're right," I said, "because in either case it's superstition. I don't think luck has anything to do with it."

We decided we would fish on opposite sides of the pond from each other. That way we could see each other and signal our progress. Sammy had always favored the side of the pond with the life-size statue of an elephant, so I told him I'd take the other side.

SIX

We set out from home two hours early the day of the contest, which meant we'd have plenty of time to pick out a spot of our choice. As it turned out we weren't the first ones there, but it didn't really matter because everyone was wandering around and no one had fixed their place as yet.

Sammy and I parted. He went over to the elephant and climbed up and stood on its back. "What do you see?" I shouted.

"Nothing," Sammy shouted back.

"Then get down before you break your neck." Sammy sat down on the elephant's back and then slowly slid off.

I had sat down on the high bank overlooking the pond. It was a hot day, no breeze, and when I looked up at the clock on the big animal den I saw that we had a full hour and a half to go.

There were usually ducks sleeping on the bank, their heads tucked under their wings, but they must have known it was the third of July because they were in the middle of the pond, along with the geese, swimming restlessly in circles. It wouldn't be long, I knew, before they'd fly to the other pond.

My eye kept going to the bridge, and it was several minutes before I realized that there was something stirring in me that I hadn't yet nailed down well enough to understand. Suddenly a voice inside me said, "That's where you've got to fish." Although I was confused by my own statement, I got to my feet and started off in the direction of the bridge.

To my surprise—probably because I had been dreaming—there was a strange girl my age very near the spot I was headed for. I'd never seen her before. I edged around her into the last available spot between her and the bridge. The girl looked at me and screwed up her freckled face, which made two brown ovals on her cheeks. "This is my spot!" she commanded.

"That's right," I said. "You haven't moved."

"That doesn't give you a right to stand on top of me."

"I'm not standing on top of you—and I'm not touching you. I guess you know the rules."

"I guess you know the rules, too—I hope," she said.

I sat down and watched her wave her pole in the air. I rejected three or four choice remarks and lay back on the grass. I closed my eyes. "This is it," I said to myself. "The great day is here. I hope I win the spinning rod, and if I can't win it myself I hope Sammy does. I promise not to brag if I win it or become jealous if Sammy wins it." That was a pretty high order, which was why I made myself promise.

SEVEN

They had waved the flag. The poles were in the water. There must have been a hundred kids in the contest, all boys except for the creature standing next to me. I couldn't decide if she was bad luck or not, so I made a point of being the last one to put his line in the water. I figured if she was bad luck this would cancel it out. I spit on my bait for extra measure.

I no sooner got my line in the water when my nextdoor neighbor pulled out her first bluegill. She took it off her hook, dropped it in her bucket, and turned and winked at me. I didn't get it. Was she bragging, was she being friendly, was she being cute, or what?

I couldn't help but notice that she was fishing without a cork. She had a single split shot about five inches up from her hook. I noticed that she retrieved her line very slowly, sometimes stopping altogether. She must have gotten the first one that way, because as I watched I noticed she got another hit. She set the hook a little too soon this time and it got away. She knew her stuff, all right, and I guess she had been letting me know with her wink.

I looked up to see Sammy hauling one in across the pond. Small. Then I got my first bite. The cork hardly rippled the water at first, but all at once it started to drift out—then it went under. I set the hook and had him. He was a good six inches. Probably the biggest one to be caught so far, which didn't mean much, but I guess it meant something.

By now the girl next to me had caught four little ones. She had lost all interest in me, and I was willing to lose all interest in her. She was obviously hoping to catch as many as she could and hope the law of averages was on her side. I was hoping for something else, but I didn't have a plan. Not yet.

I kept eyeing the bridge, and every time I did my eye would travel down to the water, and then my imagination would go down deep *into* the water, where I figured a big fish or two or three were lurking about in the shadows. I didn't have any trouble imagining a fourteen-inch bluegill down there. But I wouldn't need to catch one nearly that big to win the contest. Besides, a fourteen-inch fish would have broken my pole.

Last year the winning fish went nine and a quarter inches, a record. All the other winners had been under nine inches. In fact, the first year the winning fish was just under eight inches. Everyone said the fish were getting bigger since the contest began because the more fish we caught, the more food there was for the ones that were left.

This kind of thinking was doing me absolutely no good. I looked over at the clock. The first hour had gone by. Only one hour to go. I had caught seven fish. The first one was still the biggest. The girl beside me had at least twelve by now, and I almost let myself start wondering if she would win the weight contest, which would probably be good for a tackle box loaded with stuff. "Let her. What's it to me?" I said under my breath. "Second prize is definitely not what you had in mind," the voice concluded, just to remind me, in case I'd forgotten my goal.

EIGHT

Forty-five minutes to go.

Thirty minutes to go.

I removed my bobber, reached into my can, took out a worm, and put it in my shirt pocket.

It's now or never. Even if no one else knows where the big fish are in this pond, I do. They're right there, in the hole under the bridge. So what was holding me back: fear, embarrassment, stupidity? Yes, and one more thing besides: the rules. If you stepped into the water, even by accident, you were disqualified, and I knew it wouldn't be possible to stand on the bank next to the bridge without slipping into the water. By now I was inching my way over—that is, inching along with my feet. But even with sneakers on, my feet began to slide on the grass. Without planning to I got down on my hands and knees and started crawling, but by the time I got nearly to the edge of the bridge I started sliding again. So I did the only thing I could: I crawled on my stomach until my hands had nearly reached the water's edge. Somehow I managed to fling the line up over my head, but when I brought it down, my pole slapped the water and made a noise that could be heard from one end of the pond to the other.

The freckle-faced girl started screaming at once. "He's cheating! He's cheating!"

"There's nothing in the rule books about standing or sitting," I screamed back.

"How about crawling?" she shouted back.

"Crawling neither," I hollered.

I had caught the time out of the corner of my eye: ten minutes before two. All eyes were on me but no one else had said a word.

Just then I felt a tug, and when I looked at my pole I could see the tip being pulled toward the bridge—and I could feel a fish on the line. I gave a jerk as best I could in the position I was in, but what happened next almost stopped my breath. *I couldn't pull my pole out of the water.* The weight at the other end was too great. At first I thought I had a shark or a whale on the line—or maybe a fourteen-inch bluegill—but then I knew what it was: the fish had pulled my line under the wire fence, and instead of setting the hook, as I had thought, I had pulled it out of his mouth and my hook had caught in the mesh wiring.

I jerked and jerked, but nothing happened. By now I was lying on my side, and I thought to turn my head and look at the clock. It was five minutes before two. I pulled my pole, hand over hand until I had the line in my grasp, and I began pulling it as hard as I could. If I lost too much of my line I wouldn't have time to restring another, and so I prayed that the hook would break off. And that's what happened. Lying on my back, I reached inside my pocket, took out my extra cork, pulled off one of the hooks, reached into my shirt pocket and got my worm.

This was it, two minutes to go. If I missed the next one—if there was a next one—I would be out of time. But they were there, and they hadn't been fished for before. *And so here I go,* I said under my breath, as I flipped my pole over my head while rolling over on my stomach.

Seconds went by and nothing happened—and once again I felt the tug and could see my pole being jerked at the tip as the fish made its way under the bridge with my bait in its mouth. *Last chance, don't panic,* I told myself, as I held out till the last possible moment before setting the hook. This time I had the fish, not the fence, and I knew it. He was on—and he was BIG!

But now what? How was I to get him in? First on my back, and then on my stomach, I tried to pull him in over my head, but I just couldn't get the leverage I needed. I had to crawl for it, back the way I came. But would there be time? I looked up at the clock. Less than a minute to go. Old freckle-face saw me eyeing the clock. "You'll never make it, you'll never make it!"

It looked like my time was up but I couldn't be sure. I went faster, faster—and at last I reached level ground. Pulling with all my might, I watched as my fish broke water—just as the white flag began to wave from across the pond. And all at once a cheer went up. I was sure I had won! I had won!

"That's a record," I heard the girl saying. "I knew you could do it."

When I looked up from my beached fish—which had to be at least ten inches—I heard Sammy hollering in the distance. I looked up to see him waving his arms and running as fast as he could in my direction.

GLOSSARY

The **pronunciation** of each word in this glossary is shown by a phonetic respelling in brackets; for example, [in′sə·lāt′ing]. An accent mark (′) follows the syllable with the most stress: [ə·blāz′]. A secondary, or lighter, accent mark (′) follows a syllable with less stress: [bloo͞o′gil′]. The key to other pronunciation symbols is below. You will find a shortened version of this key on alternate pages of the glossary.

Pronunciation Key*

a	add, map	m	move, seem	u	up, done
ā	ace, rate	n	nice, tin	û(r)	burn, term
â(r)	care, air	ng	ring, song	yoo͞	fuse, few
ä	palm, father	o	odd, hot	v	vain, eve
b	bat, rub	ō	open, so	w	win, away
ch	check, catch	ô	order, jaw	y	yet, yearn
d	dog, rod	oi	oil, boy	z	zest, muse
e	end, pet	ou	pout, now	zh	vision, pleasure
ē	equal, tree	o͝o	took, full	ə	the schwa,
f	fit, half	o͞o	pool, food		an unstressed
g	go, log	p	pit, stop		vowel representing
h	hope, hate	r	run, poor		the sound spelled
i	it, give	s	see, pass		a in *above*
ī	ice, write	sh	sure, rush		e in *sicken*
j	joy, ledge	t	talk, sit		i in *possible*
k	cool, take	th	thin, both		o in *melon*
l	look, rule	t̶h̶	this, bathe		u in *circus*

ancient

banner

biscuit *Bis-* or *bi-* at the beginning of a word often means "two." *Bicycle*, for example, means "a cycle with two wheels." *Bis-* in *biscuit* means "two" also. *Cuit* is a French word meaning "cooked." A *biscuit* is "bread cooked two times" until it is hard and dry. The first *biscuits* were like the crackers that we eat today.

A

a·ban·doned [ə·ban'dənd] *adj.* Left all alone: **We think the baby bird was** *abandoned*, **because no other birds have helped it.**

a·blaze [ə·blāz'] *adj.* On fire, or appearing to be on fire: **The room was** *ablaze* **with light from all the candles.**

ac·count [ə·kount'] *n.* Story, or explanation: **My dad's** *account* **of the day he won his hero's medal always makes me feel proud.** *syn.* version

an·cient [ān'shənt] *adj.* From long, long ago: **Two thousand years ago, in the** *ancient* **city of Rome, the people spoke the Latin language.**

B

ban·ner [ban'ər] *n.* A long piece of cloth with words printed on it that is hung up or held out for many people to see: **Our class hung a** *banner* **with "Let There Be Peace on Earth" printed on it.**

bar·gain [bär'gən] *n.* A special deal to buy something for less money than it usually costs: **The desk lamp was a** *bargain* **because a lamp that nice usually costs much more.**

birch [bûrch] *n.* A hardwood tree with thin bark that peels off easily: **The bark of** *birches* **can be made into useful things like baskets.**

bis·cuit [bis'kit] *n.* A type of flaky bread, baked in small cakes: **My dad baked** *biscuits* **this morning, and I put jam on them.**

block [blok] *n.* A square area of buildings with four streets around it: **There are apartment buildings, stores, and a few houses on the** *block* **where I live.**

blue·gill [blōō'gil'] *n.* A type of sunfish found in fresh water, such as ponds, rivers, and lakes, not in saltwater oceans: **The** *bluegills* **my mom is cooking for dinner are the same fish my dad caught in the lake this morning.**

bril·liant [bril′yənt] *adj.*
Very bright: **The stars are easy to see because they are *brilliant* tonight.**

buck·skin [buk′skin′] *n.* A material made from the skin of deer or sheep: **My uncle has a beautiful jacket made of *buckskin*.**

coun·cil [koun′səl] *adj.*
Having to do with a meeting of the members of a group or club who come together to discuss something: **The members of the club sat at the *council* table to plan how to teach water safety to children.**

coast

C

char·coal [chär′kōl′] *n.* A black substance made of burned wood: **The fire has stopped burning, and the trees are mostly *charcoal* now.**

coast [kōst] *n.* The land at the edge of a body of water, such as an ocean: **The old house was built on the hill above the rocky *coast* of the Atlantic Ocean.** *syn.* shore

col·lec·tion [kə·lek′shən] *n.* A group of the same kinds of things, gathered by someone: **Lara had a *collection* of toy dogs.**

cor·du·roy [kôr′də·roi] *adj.* Made of strong cotton cloth that has raised ridges: ***Corduroy* clothes are warm and feel soft.**

D

din·er [dī′nər] *n.* A type of restaurant that looks like the long, narrow dining car of a train: **I sat in a booth at the end of the long room of the *diner* and ordered a sandwich.**

E

ex·traor·di·nar·y [ik·strôr′də·ner′ē *or* ek′strə·ôr′də·ner′ē] *adj.* Special; unusual; far beyond the ordinary: **Our *extraordinary* sewing class made fifty blankets to give to needy people, which is more than any other class has ever made.**

corduroy Did you know that when you put on clothes made of *corduroy* you are wearing something fit for a king? *Corduroy* was once woven from silk thread and used only by the kings of France for their hunting outfits. The word comes to us from the French phrase *corde du roi*, which means "cloth of the king."

a	add	o͞o	took
ā	ace	o͞o	pool
â	care	u	up
ä	palm	û	burn
e	end	yo͞o	fuse
ē	equal	oi	oil
i	it	ou	pout
ī	ice	ng	ring
o	odd	th	thin
ō	open	th	this
ô	order	zh	vision

ə = { a in *above* e in *sicken*
i in *possible*
o in *melon* u in *circus*

footbridge

foot·bridge [foot′brij′] *n.* A small bridge built for people to walk across, not drive across: **Carmen walked across the *footbridge* to join Bill on the other side of the creek.**

glint [glint] *n.* A bright flash like light; or an expression showing sudden feeling: **Her eyes seemed to light up with a *glint* of humor.**

grid·dle [grid′(ə)l] *n.* A flat pan used to cook food on top of a stove or fire: **Karen could smell the pancakes cooking on the *griddle*.**

griddle

insulating Two thousand years ago the Roman people spoke a language called Latin. The Latin word for "island" was *insula*. Much later, English borrowed *insula* to make the word *insulate*. When you are *insulating* an object, you are surrounding it with something to keep out heat or cold. In fact, you are turning that object into a kind of *island*.

in·su·lat·ing [in′sə·lāt′ing] *adj.* Keeping something warm or cold: **The sleeping bag I use when I go camping is made of *insulating* fabric so I won't get cold at night.**

jin·gle [jing′gəl] *v.* **jin·gled, jin·gling** To sound something like bells; tinkle: **The coins *jingled* in Anna's pocket when she ran.** *syn.* clink

keel [kēl] *v.* To fall to the ground because you are hurt or tired: **Jean had been dancing for hours and said she would *keel* over if she danced to one more song.**

leath·er [leth′ər] *adj.* Made from animal skin: **Cowhands wear *leather* pants made from cowhide to protect their legs.**

maid·en [mād′(ə)n] *n.* A young unmarried woman: **The young *maiden* in the tale was happy to see the prince.**

mis·chief [mis′chif] *n.* Sneaky actions that can cause something bad to happen: **Derek was into *mischief* when he hid Clara's library books so she couldn't return them.** *syn.* prank

mur·mur [mûr′mər] *v.* **mur·mured, mur·mur·ing** To speak in a low, somewhat unclear voice: **Anita *murmured* so softly that I couldn't hear her.**

non·sense [non′sens] *n.* Silly words or actions: **Carlos said his cat flies when it jumps, but I told him that was *nonsense*.** *syn.* foolishness

orb [ôrb] *n.* A circular shape like a ball: **The moon is a shiny yellow *orb* in the night sky.**

or·i·gin [ôr′ə·jin] *n.* The beginning of something: **The ancient Latin language is the *origin* of many English words.**

o·val [ō′vəl] *n.* A rounded but long shape, like an egg: **The earrings were white *ovals*, so Francie thought they looked like tiny eggs.**

pace [pās] *n.* Rate of speed, from slow to fast: **I walk three miles a week at a fast *pace* to have a healthy heart.**

patch·work [pach′wûrk′] *adj.* Made of many pieces of different cloth sewn together in a design: **Wendy is making a *patchwork* tablecloth from fabric scraps.**

plaid [plad] *n.* A pattern on cloth with stripes of different colors that cross each other: **The warm blanket is green, black, and blue *plaid*.**

praise [prāz] *n.* Good things said about something or someone: **Lily received *praises* from me for doing so well.**

pred·a·tor [pred′ə·tər] *n.* An animal that eats other animals: **Lions and tigers are *predators* on the African grasslands.**

oval If you believe that something *oval* is shaped like an egg, you are not the first person to think so. The word for "egg" in the Latin language spoken two thousand years ago was *ovum*. From this word came the English word *oval*.

patchwork

predator

a	add	o͞o	took
ā	ace	o͞o	pool
â	care	u	up
ä	palm	û	burn
e	end	y͞oo	fuse
ē	equal	oi	oil
i	it	ou	pout
ī	ice	ng	ring
o	odd	th	thin
ō	open	th	this
ô	order	zh	vision

ə = { a in *above*   e in *sicken*
       i in *possible*
       o in *melon*   u in *circus* }

reed

sea urchin

prowl [proul] *v.* **prowled, prowl·ing** To move quietly and carefully in search of food: **The tiger was *prowling* around the jungle, looking for something to eat.** *syn.* stalk

Q

quilt [kwilt] *n.* A bedcover made of warm material stitched between two layers of cloth: **The *quilt* kept me warm in my bed on chilly winter nights.**

R

reed [rēd] *n.* Tall, thin grass that is hollow like a straw and grows in wet places: **The geese make their nests in the *reeds* near the lake.**

re·ha·bil·i·ta·tion [rē'hə·bil'ə·tā'shən] *n.* The task of bringing something back to normal after it has been hurt: **Paul went to the hospital for *rehabilitation* after he hurt his leg.**

re·past [ri·past'] *n.* A meal: **The travelers had their morning *repast* of juice and muffins in the hotel restaurant.**

res·cued [res'kyo͞od] *adj.* Saved from some danger: **The sailors from the *rescued* ship thanked the woman who saved them.**

rip·ple [rip'əl] *v.* **rip·pled, rip·pling** To move like little waves: **The sheets on the clothesline *rippled* in the wind.**

S

scoff [skof *or* skôf] *v.* **scoffed, scoff·ing** To tease someone about something he or she says is true: **The boys *scoffed* at Marcos when he said he could fix the broken radio, but he fixed it.** *syn.* mock

sea ur·chin [sē'ûr'chin] *n.* A small sea animal whose round body is covered with spines: **Felipe tried to pick up the *sea urchins* he saw at the beach, but their spines were too sharp to touch.**

spe·cial·ty [spesh′əl·tē] *n.* A special or well-made thing, especially an item someone is very good at making: **My dad is a wonderful cook, and one of his** *specialties* **is cake.**

sum·mons [sum′ənz] *n.* A call or invitation to someone to come to a place, especially to a very important meeting: **We received a** *summons* **to the principal's office to tell him about our project.**

sur·vey [sər·vā′] *v.* **sur·veyed, sur·vey·ing** To look over all of something: **Don was** *surveying* **the field, looking for yellow butterflies.**

tex·ture [teks′chər] *n.* The feel of a fabric: **My new jeans and shirt had rough** *textures* **until I washed them to make them soft.**

tim·id [tim′id] *adj.* Shy and a little afraid: **The little boy is so** *timid* **he looks down and hides behind his mother when people talk to him.** *syn.* bashful

un·der·wa·ter [un′dər·wô′tər *or* un′dər·wo′tər] *adj.* Used, found, or done below the surface of the water: **People can take pictures of fish with** *underwater* **cameras.**

vel·vet [vel′vit] *n.* A very soft cloth that feels smooth and a little fuzzy: **The dress was made of lovely purple** *velvet* **that was as soft as flower petals.**

texture

underwater

wave·length [wāv′leng(k)th′] *n.* Thoughts or feelings similar to another person's: **My best friend and I think so much alike that it seems we are usually on the same** *wavelength.*

a	add	o͝o	took
ā	ace	o͞o	pool
â	care	u	up
ä	palm	û	burn
e	end	yo͞o	fuse
ē	equal	oi	oil
i	it	ou	pout
ī	ice	ng	ring
o	odd	th	thin
ō	open	th	this
ô	order	zh	vision

ə = { a in *above* e in *sicken*
　　 i in *possible*
　　 o in *melon* u in *circus*

INDEX OF
TITLES AND AUTHORS

Page numbers in light printed letters refer to information about the author.